EARTH

Poems

CECILIA WOLOCH

Winner of the 2014 Two Sylvias Press Chapbook Prize

Two Sylvias Press

Two Sylvias Press
PO Box 1524
Kingston, WA 98346
twosylviaspress@gmail.com

Cover Art: *Crossed Tails* by Jonde Northcutt
Cover Design: Kelli Russell Agodon
Book Design: Annette Spaulding-Convy

Created with the belief that **great writing is good for the world**, Two Sylvias Press mixes modern technology, classic style, and literary intellect with an eco-friendly heart. We draw our inspiration from the poetic literary talent of Sylvia Plath and the editorial business sense of Sylvia Beach. We are an independent press dedicated to publishing the exceptional voices of writers.

For more information about Two Sylvias Press or to learn more about the eBook version of *Earth* please visit: www.twosylviaspress.com

First Edition. Created in the United States of America.

ISBN: 13: 978-0692333372
ISBN: 10: 0692333371

Two Sylvias Press
www.twosylviaspress.com

Praise For *Earth*

In *Earth*, Cecilia Woloch writes with the wonder and resilience that are essential, not only to empathy, but to transformation. Woloch weds us to the natural world through language that is both straightforward and particular. A "river's lifting dress" comes to represent history; branches swaying "like the arms of a woman waving goodbye" come to represent mortality. These remarkable poems are hymns and requiems; they are made of "blood mixed with earth." —Terrance Hayes

~

These poems reflect a mature writer, a woman unflinching in both love and craft. The love is unabashed; the language boldly lyrical and image-rich. As a devoted reader of Cecilia Woloch's writing, I relish anything she offers, so I welcome *Earth,* this book of passionate, vigorous poetry, in which grandeur of spirit always redeems sorrow. As Woloch writes in the gorgeous prose poem "Afterlife": "I want to be fierce and joyful and a meadow when I'm dead." May we all be meadows with you, Dear Poet. —Holly Prado

~

These poems gel together beautifully with a musical sense of foreboding and epiphany inhabiting the lines. These pages give us a terrain where a "honey of birdcall in our mouth" seems equally at place with a landscape populated with a willow that leaves the speaker "half afraid that the tree would fly." I want to return to *Earth* again and again. —Aimee Nezhukumatathil

Acknowledgements

Some of these poems first appeared in the following journals and magazines. Many thanks to the editors.

Indiana Review: "2006"

Cave Wall: "What Was Promised Me" and "Our Father in the Last Gold Light of Spring"

Crab Orchard Review: "Teta" and "Afterlife"

Mississippi Review: "Your River"

Double Room: "Wild Common Prayer"

Bright Wings: An Illustrated Anthology of Poems About Birds, edited by Billy Collins: "For the Birds"

Spoon River Poetry Review: "Harry and Pearl: A Villanelle"

Asheville Poetry Review: "Little Song for the One Afraid" and "Earth"

Double Room: "Wild Common Prayer"

American Mustard: "My Face" and "A Place in the Music"

Love and gratitude to Holly Prado and her Tuesday morning writing workshop for ongoing support and encouragement, and to Carine Topal and Sarah Luczaj for their invaluable feedback on work-in-progress.

TABLE OF CONTENTS

I.

What Was Promised Me   1

Teta   2

Her Tree   5

Little Song For The One Afraid   6

My Face   7

A Place In The Music   8

2006   9

Earth   10

II.

Your River   13

Wild Common Prayer   14

For The Birds   15

Our Father, In The Last Gold Light Of Spring   17

Ghost Sycamore   19

Harry & Pearl: A Villanelle   21

My Mother Is The Poem I'll Never Write   23

Afterlife   25

For my mother, in memory

Tell me there is
A meadow, afterward.

— Lucie Brock-Broido

I.

WHAT WAS PROMISED ME

Nothing. A ring and some salt. Rice in the white shoes. Music. A doll. The book my mother read to me, over and over, when I was a child: tigers turning to butter, to milk. An amulet from a boy who carried a knife in his pocket, too. Night — I was not promised dawn — stars hooked to sky by my father's hands. Love like a tree I could climb to the top of and then jump down from, or swing from, or fly. Mercies so small I could hide each one inside a flower. Sharp white teeth. A clock made of pearls, each pearl an hour, and the hours numberless. The pink dress that disappeared — where did it go? — and the tiny ballerina spinning and spinning inside a dome. A door that would open and close. No house. No home but the story I've lived toward. Luck running out like a shimmer of wind. Two buckets full of cold water, wood for a fire, and flame.

TETA

for my great-aunt

Teta, it's winter in Pittsburgh again
— darkbrick city of smokestacks and soot —
and we're walking up Broadway Avenue,
past billboards and vacant lots,
through the slush of snow and cinders
as the streetcars slur past — ghosts
in our flowered babushkas and shabby coats,
shopping bags weighing down our arms.

We've bought cans of beets, heads of cabbage,
meat ground fresh that we'll squeeze into fists,
and we don't flinch when the crew-cut kids hiss,
D.P.'s, at our backs; we're not ashamed anymore, at last,
to have come from nowhere, nothing, dirt —
the village you fled as a young girl, gone,
the houses burned and the fields you worked
into rows of green grown wild again.

Once you spooned honey into my mouth
because my arms and legs were *like sticks,*
because I itched and wept and wanted,
more than sweetness, to know who I was.
But you sighed, *No one wants to remember that stuff —*

how you came to this new country, stinking of ship;

how you sold bootleg hootch for cash,

your own smooth flesh for a rich man's song —

the fat growing fat on the fat of the land

while you buried one child in a pauper's grave,

raised two others on blood money, prayer.

All your sins in a basket too heavy to lift

and your body already a heap of grief

the day you slipped in the alley and fell

in that garden you'd made of ground bone, ash,

under a slit of tin-washed sky.

And then you never stood up again.

I watched as you shrank in your narrow bed,

blind, but you gripped my hand and sang

the old song of the little bird in a tongue

I still don't understand — dark syllables fluttering

just out of reach — until you were shadow, whisper,

less —your whole life a ragged story

stitched into breath, unstitched again.

Teta, we've never been much in this world,

although we were many, too many, once —

the children's children who circled your table,

blowing out candles, eyes tilted like yours;

our faces the same face all over again,

the face of the stranger wherever we turned —

my cousin the Cossack, the Gypsy, the Jew;

my cousin the dark Slav, my cousin the slave.

And we'll never belong to this place

where you came with your one suitcase

tied with rope, with your shape like a shadow

risen from earth — some mute root pulled

from a meadow where wildflowers blazed

in the summer and winter lay down.

This is America, Teta, you're dead,

and our dying means nothing here.

Give me your bags.

HER TREE

There was a tree I loved and had always loved. *Silver willow*, I heard it was called. I called it *Grandmother-as-a-Girl*. I called it *Grandmother-Under-the-Ground*. I waded the river beneath its shade, my feet in the cool, shallow water, then lay in the sunlight to listen for her. When the storm crossed the meadow — a sudden darkening; great ships of clouds racing overhead — each leaf of my grandmother's tree turned its shimmering back to the breeze; each leaf a tongue to the rain, many-tongued. I stood up in the wind and ran through the high grass, as if through a sea of light. Half afraid that the tree would fly, but I turned to look and the tree didn't budge. Its branches only swayed like the arms of a woman waving good-bye. A woman who'd stood in the doorway, once, of a house that would burn to the ground when she'd gone, shaking the crumbs from her apron for birds. A woman I knew would die too young, earth in her mouth, and keep calling me back. I reached the road with my arms full of wildflowers, weeds, one twig I'd snapped from a branch. All this I saved for an altar, a grave. Drenched in the sky — gray, then silver, then green.

LITTLE SONG FOR THE ONE AFRAID

Oh beloved, oh afraid
of the bloodstain, dark spot, ticking clock
of what has shone in your life like luck —
too bright to last — oh fortunate
who slipped the licked stones, glittering
inside your pockets, spread your arms
and dreamt your ghost wings would unfurl
from your bony shoulders — *angel bones* —
and that the sky would hold you up
and love — a tree from which you swung —
oh branch you called your father's name
oh bird who sang your mother's song
oh little sweeper of the world
whose life inside my life has burned.

MY FACE

I thought I'd grow up to be a fish. Or a tree, or a piece of wind, like God. I thought I'd scrape against myself until my face became my face. I never thought I'd grow up to look like my mother, much as I craved her one pink dress, stuttered around in her high heeled shoes, tried to sing the songs she sang. Or like my father, with his shadow in his shadow, pockets, keys. I planted tulips upside down, thinking those flowers would bloom in hell, and that hell was deep inside the earth. I walked around when I was small and spit my name into my hands. I wanted everything to shine. But I was dark. And could not swim.

A PLACE IN THE MUSIC

Once, in a dream that wasn't a dream, I saw them walking away from me. Or not away, but just ahead. All my dead beloveds in a shiver of silvery wind. They knew I was following, and kept on. Arms linked, walking side-by-side on a road between fields of waist-high grass. The wind tossing their hair and the hems of the flowered dresses the women wore. Some uncle or other, still a boy, running after the rest — was that joy? And what it said to me, this picture in my mind, was to not be afraid: that it's only a kind of magic, death, and the story is rich, the story goes on. I was behind them, watching them walk into the wind, when I heard the hum beginning inside me— a place in the music, high and sweet — as if they were singing or also heard the song I'd begun to hear, and were glad. And loved me still. The sky that silver, too. Although none of them turned around.

2006

In the year of the poppy year of the cornflower

year of the meadow of yarrow and buttercup

year of the thistle and ox-eyed daisy

in the spring of the year of our lord

of the train the engine the ticket the map

of the landscape of leaf shadow willow white birch

blurring past in the smoke of the burning fields

in the blue mist of evening the ringing of bells

ringing out for the living the living the dead

of the last great war which is one long war

of the ancient soldier come in his uniform

to stand hopefully at the door

of the house of no mirrors swept of ash

(in which I was a guest of the dark bread and rain)

to ask, *Have the Germans already left?*

sixty years after the forests were flushed

of the last of our enemies last of the partisans

of the holy republic of mud

of the blood mixed with earth of the bones of itself

of which no one knows but the trees anymore

of which no one speaks but the child made of grass.

EARTH

We've traveled like this all our lives, all our life as a people on the earth. We've gathered and scattered and gathered again. In rooms made of firelight or of song. We've buried our dead, when we could, in places they loved, or the bones of them. Every step, a turn of the wheel, a word set down and no other word; every turn of the wheel a prayer in mud, the answer of one God. Sometimes we've veiled ourselves and sometimes we've stood, clothed only in sunlight and wind. Sugar of flowers on our breath; honey of birdcall in our mouths. Once, I'd forgotten the way to the well and the smell of cool rain led me there. Once I was only a child in my sleep; then I awoke and was everywhere.

II.

YOUR RIVER

for Eve, on the Chattahoochee

Your river has wish in it, and rain
and mud and twigs and the trees' lost leaves.

Oh, it's not really your river, but still
you widow it, walk beside it some.

Your dogs think the river is theirs,
bark at the birds and fish, swim sticks

across where it's deepest in their mouths.
It's not really their river, but nights

they breathe the dark house at its bend asleep.
As the green barn dreams your gone love's dreams —

joist and beam, the sweet machines
in their sweet repose of weeds and rust

— oh wheel, oh hope, oh grass grown deep.
Today I circled the meadow, a hawk

in the river's lifted dress, this wind.

WILD COMMON PRAYER

for SLS

I dreamt you were whole again, radiant, calm: your hair still golden but tinged with red — a halo of rosy, burnished light — and your hands untrembling in your lap. I was surprised to find you home. *But I've been here all along,* you said. Or might have said. You didn't speak. You'd only aged as women age whose bodies ease them toward death; grown softer, more yourself. And I was the one who stood amazed, there in the kitchen where we'd spent so many quiet mornings, friend. Wanting to touch you, wanting to simply not forsake you now. Outside, the pasture lay down calmly; each blade shimmered in the wind. *This is eternity,* I thought, and felt you breaking into all your lovely fragments as I woke.

FOR THE BIRDS

I stopped under a sycamore, looked up:
bare white limbs against blue, blue sky
and in those branches, flickering, birds,
each with a bright green-yellow breast,
each the size of a small child's fist.
So what kind of birds are you? I asked

and slipped on my glasses, the better to glimpse
such wing and color, such flashiness.
Then, breathless, I climbed the sun-swept hill
to the naturalists' offices, rushed inside,
saying, *I have a question about a bird!*
and was handed a book of birds to check.

I considered *Common Yellow Throat* —
Skulks in marshes. Male wears black mask.
Wichity-wichity song — loved that music,
but wondered if music could be the answer
to anything? I leafed through a few more pages,
learned that American Goldfinches turn

from winter's muddy greenish-brown
to summer's yellow brightness, turn
betwixt, in spring, this lemon-lime

and fly *in hiccups*, flash their gold, a flock

of such birds being called *a charm*,

from the Latin *carmen*, meaning *song*.

I flew back down the hill in that windy light

practically into the sycamore's arms,

singing, anyway, *skulks in marshes,*

black mask, wichity-wichity song!

Singing, *Spread out your colors, flash me your wings* —

as the charm made its green-yellow sweep through the sky.

OUR FATHER, IN THE LAST GOLD LIGHT OF SPRING

says to me, *Take down your hands.*

Says, *Let your sister have it, if she wants.*
Wants nothing now.

The light that stood behind him will not stand.
So summer comes.

So he has not stood up in years,
who was the last of something, once.

Who once swam through flames, I thought.
Who made a shadow like a bird.

What do I want to know, and can't?
That what he'd never said, he said.

That he'd kept his ankles covered where the chains
had gnawed his skin.

That he'd planted corn and melons
near the creek beside the house.

That the leafy golden light behind him

darkened. It was June.

GHOST SYCAMORE

The winter I knew you weren't coming back,
I ran down the hill from the house, the path

through the woods turning red and gold with death
— dank leaves underfoot; branches twined overhead —

and, breathless, stopped where the lake begins,
having glimpsed, through the tangled mist, a glint

of something glimmering, silvery, bright —
I stepped from the shadows toward that shine

and suddenly, there, in the sky at my feet
on the lake's surface, shimmering, a tree —

or the ghost of a white tree, lightning-limbed,
that seemed to have risen up from within

the body of water, the body of sky —
and again, on the far shore, the other side,

the same tree — spectral, luminous —
bowed as in grief at the water's edge

where it stood among lush pines, bone-white, stark
— stripped of leaves, of rough outer bark —

old sycamore, old boundary-marker — father,
as I saw you in a dream, once, self and other

self, in this world and the next, as if a veil
between them lifted, then everything went still.

HARRY & PEARL: A VILLANELLE

My father wears shoes in the afterworld
— the shiny, brown dress shoes we buried him in.
My mother goes barefoot and answers to *Pearl*

though that wasn't her name. Daddy called her *girl*
and told us, *Your mother works hard; be good kids.*
Now Daddy wears shoes in the afterworld

because he lay shoeless his last years, lay curled
like a child in his bed crying out, or he'd sing
and our mother went barefoot and answered him. *Pearl*

was her middle name, given her, slurred, at birth
— a drunken grand uncle's grandiose gift.
But our father wears shoes in the afterworld

and our mother, who followed him — ever his jewel —
to wherever they've gone, in her last white dress
goes barefoot beside him now, answers to *Pearl*

— won't answer to *mother* and won't be implored;
she cooked and she cleaned and she sang *that's enough.*
Now my father wears shoes in the afterworld

— shiny brown dress shoes — and gives her a twirl
in his arms, she's his girl, she's his girl again, laughs —
my mother, who's barefoot and answers to *Pearl*

when I call to her, call to my sweet disappeared
mother and father who slipped through my breath.
My father wears shoes in the afterworld.
My mother goes barefoot and answers to *Pearl*.

MY MOTHER IS THE POEM I'LL NEVER WRITE

When I hated myself,

when I sulked and bled

and had no god to call,

she loved me;

she called me back.

Her strength was the wren's

plain strength

but my mother was beautiful,

more beautiful than I saw,

more delicate.

Really, I don't want to tell anyone.

What's to tell?

Her crooked hands.

When I was hungry,

I was fed.

When I was sad,

I could lie down

beside her in her bed,

or when I was glad,

exhausted from joy

from working beside her

in the garden

or in the kitchen

she swept and swept.

When I had wrecked my life,

she told me, *You don't have to*

fall apart.

When I was wrong

she taught me

how to forgive myself.

When she died

I took the flowers from her grave

and scattered them.

When I want her voice,

her face again,

I have only

to look in the mirror.

Gone like the sparrow,

gone like the wren.

Gone like the blossoms

blown into drifts

from which her name

was gathered once.

AFTERLIFE

I want to be fierce and joyful and a meadow when I'm dead. Spindly flowers and waist-high grass and the shadows of clouds across that brightness, shifting, like so many ships in the sky. I want to be all in one place, at last, but vast, a sea by the side of the road. I mean green, and I mean poppies and daisies, everything blooming at once. And I want to be, again, that girl who pushed into the wind. Who stood up to the sun, big-mouthed and brave. I mean, if I'm going to die, let me live. Let me wade out into the darkest part of the night and name myself. Wild-haired bitch of the mongrel stars. Moon on her shoulders. Dirt-rich, proud.

Cecilia Woloch is the author of six collections of poems, most recently *Carpathia* (BOA Editions 2009). The French translation of her second book, *Tsigan: The Gypsy Poem*, was published as *Tzigane: le poeme gitane* by Scribe-l'Harmattan in 2014. *Tsigan* has also been adapted for multi-media performances in the U.S. and Europe. Her novella, *Sur la Route*, a finalist for the Colony Collapse Prize, is forthcoming from Quale Press in 2015. Other literary honors include The Indiana Review Prize for Poetry, The New Ohio Review Prize for Poetry, the Scott Russell Sanders Prize for Creative Nonfiction, and fellowships from the National Endowment for the Arts, the California Arts Council, CEC/ArtsLink International, Chateau de la Napoule Foundation, the Center for International Theatre Development and many others. She collaborates regularly with musicians, dancers, visual artists, theatre artists and filmmakers. The founding director of Summer Poetry in Idyllwild and The Paris Poetry Workshop, she has also served on the faculties of a number of creative writing programs and teaches independently throughout the U.S. and around the world.

Publications by Two Sylvias Press:

The Daily Poet: Day-By-Day Prompts For Your Writing Practice
by Kelli Russell Agodon and Martha Silano (Print and eBook)

Fire On Her Tongue: An Anthology of Contemporary Women's Poetry
edited by Kelli Russell Agodon and Annette Spaulding-Convy (Print and eBook)

The Poet Tarot and Guidebook: A Deck Of Creative Exploration (Print)

Earth, Winner of the 2014 Two Sylvias Press Chapbook Prize (Print and eBook)
By Cecilia Woloch

The Cardiologist's Daughter
by Natasha Kochicheril Moni (Print and eBook)

She Returns to the Floating World
by Jeannine Hall Gailey (Print and eBook)

Hourglass Museum
by Kelli Russell Agodon (eBook)

Dear Alzheimer's: A Caregiver's Diary & Poems
by Esther Altshul Helfgott (eBook)

Listening to Mozart: Poems of Alzheimer's
by Esther Altshul Helfgott (eBook)

Cloud Pharmacy
by Susan Rich (eBook)

Crab Creek Review 30th Anniversary Issue featuring Northwest Poets
edited by Kelli Russell Agodon and Annette Spaulding-Convy (eBook)

Please visit Two Sylvias Press (www.twosylviaspress.com) for information on purchasing our print books, eBooks, writing tools, and for submission guidelines for our annual chapbook prize. Two Sylvias Press also offers editing services and manuscript consultations.

Created with the belief that great writing
is good for the world.

two sylvias press

Visit us online: www.twosylviaspress.com

CPSIA information can be obtained
at www.ICGtesting.com
Printed in the USA
LVOW11s1559061116

511815LV00008B/16/P